"*Newsworthy* has solved an important and difficult equation: How does one not shy away from the direct glare of these horrors and not despair? Mouton has written a collection in which the most harrowing stories interlace with the always boundless imagination of children and the music such imagination conjures. It is this imagination—even as it runs into sour realities—that frames a black resilience born of our ability to absorb, integrate, make new, redefine, and be redefined by all which meets us. She dances powerfully and smoothly while looking us in the eye, and in that work has achieved something wonderful, rare, and as old as Blackness itself. This is the collection you need if you want to be gifted new ways with which to meet and successfully tackle old demons. We owe Deborah Mouton a great debt."
—Roger Bonair Agard, performance artist and author of
Bury My Clothes

"*Newsworthy* is an honest title. This is a timely, important collection written by a powerful and urgent voice. Mouton gives us a treasure trove pregnant with polyrhythmic gems about loss, pain, death, injustice, memory, and the problems at the core of American heartbreak. Recommended? No; this is required reading."
—Gabino Iglesias, *PANK* magazine

"Deborah D.E.E.P. Mouton's *Newsworthy* is a startlingly timely collection of poems that explores the murders of Black Americans. Despite Death's ever-presence in these poems, her verse is alive, syntactically and rhythmically."
—Porsha Olayiwola, poet and activist

"Unflinchingly heartfelt—a daring, essential work."
—Tim Seibles, author of *Fast Animal*

NEWSWORTHY

Poems

Deborah D.E.E.P. Mouton

BLOOMSDAY

Published in the United States by Bloomsday

bloomsdayliterary.com

Houston, Texas

No part of this book may be reproduced, in any form, without written permission from the publisher. If you would like to use material from the book (other than for review purposes), prior written permission must be obtained by contacting the publisher. Request for permission should be e-mailed to info@bloomsdayliterary.com.

ISBN 978-0-9998239-3-4

Library of Congress Control Number 2019901691

Printed in the United States of America

FIRST EDITION

Portrait photography by Paula Nguyen Luu

Book design by Houston Creative Space

To Mother, Father, and Joshua for teaching me how to fight back

To all the families still waiting for justice

CONTENTS

3 **THE TIME WE LEARNED TO REPORT**

4 FIRST TIME AROUND THE BLOCK

7 BIRD

9 ELEVEN QUESTIONS FOR POLITICAL ASYLUM

13 **THE TIME WE WERE ALIASES**

14 BELL AND REQUIEM

15 FREAK SHOW STATION

19 **THE TIME WE WENT OVER THE EDGE**

20 SANFORD SWEET

22 SUMMONING

25 **THE TIME WE LEARNED THE RULES**

26 GAS STATION LIBRETTO

31 FILTER

33 OPEN SEASON

37 THE TIME WE WERE THUGS

39 TETRAS

41 WOLF CRY

43 KEL-TEC PF-9

45 THE TIME WE CAME CLOSE

46 WALMART WELCOME

47 A DEATH FIVE WAYS

48 ON BALTIMORE FROM BEEVILLE

50 HOUSTON TO POOL PARTY

53 THE TIME WE UNLEARNED THE RULES

54 ONE DEGREE

56 RELEASE

60 AND WE SHAKE

62 DON'T

64 THE PACT

66 PERSONAL EFFECTS

69 THE TIME WE SHOOK TO DEATH

NEWSWORTHY

The Time We Learned to Report

Summer stoop, South Central, L.A. Two children playing News.
Josh kneels behind a makeshift cardboard desk. His nine-year-
old legs finding it awkward to bend into childhood. Within
reach, a yellow Playskool tape recorder. Inside, a cassette labeled
"Summertime Jams" (MC Hammer, Ace of Base), recording tabs
taped up. Cued for erasing and re-recording. Josh broadcasts:
*Breaking news. Today a house, built by my own two hands, went up
in a ball of flames. Inside, a brave G.I. Joe tried to save Babysitter
Barbie, but it was too late. Tearjerker. Now let's go to Amandla in the
field. Amandla?* His sister, five, pushes flower barrettes from her
forehead. Spoon microphone clings to her chin. *Today the jump
rope record was broken. Again. Twenty times and counting. I did it!
I'm the be—.* Josh interrupts, says not news. Too naive. Can't see
what's important. Table shutters under silent weight. Amandla
stomps out. Whispers: *I'm gonna tell.*

> Now live from the field
> Cutouts spilling from cupped hands
> Watch the story light

First Time Around the Block

    1

    2

    3

    4 | 5

Feet syncopate

hopscotch

under ripe street lights

Sun crawls down the

backside of the mountain

We sand our hands

in four squares

on rubber balls

We bounce Sally Walker

and a cool drink of Kool-aid

powder in sugared Ziploc

till all parts of our mouths

stained cherry rebel

defiant

    6

    7

    8

    9 | 10

Streets so alive in L.A.

don't nobody want the night

to come just want the day

forever run like a highway

turn ourselves invisible
when Momma calls
> *Don't take that ball*
> *all angry*
> *The day done left*
> *you boy*

That streetlight not hot yet
ignore the glow
for the sting
of Pop Rocks in our cheeks
and Big League tiring our chew

    10 | 9
      8
      7
      6

This time
when momma calls
seems more ambulance
in her throat
more flashing light
in her eyes more
than just a halogen
flickering bulb on concrete
She says our names
like they are blood moons
in a clear sky

that no one wants to see
Like a routine turned
into red mouth outcry
A frenzy of our shadowy feet
cockroaching from the asphalt
towards our mothers'
arms unaware

     5 | 4
      3
      2
          run
The unknowing left that night
We watch their feet
turn Rodney soccer ball
Police: no longer the place to run
when lost
Police: run longer
or be a lost place
colored lips
gushing a bloody drink
more thirsty for the darkness
than the sun
and we
a chalk-outlined number
needing to be
stomped

Bird

I didn't understand the
phrase a *chicken with its
head cut off* until you

They called you Byrd
envied your strut
'round town 'nuff to wrangle it

into a pickup bed
a ride to coop,
'nother name for slaughter

To behead a bird
should be a most
humane execution

Wrung your neck
against a blind culvert
you molted over three miles
before they realized
you weren't even alive
just a headless shell
of plumage strewn over
skidmark asphalt
exhaust de-feathering your limbs

When they dropped you
in the mouth of the
cemetery
I began to crave
monster
—a delicacy for the draggable

Eleven Questions for Political Asylum

1. Hadn't you heard
   you were not an island
   Boy?

2. You were a wetback
   in a sea full of dollars?

3. Why did you smell
   so saltwater fresh
   so Côte d'Ivoire released?

4. Didn't you know how to lose
   your accent faster?

5. Didn't you know how a lone
   immigrant aches?

> *Should've called*
> *yourself transplant*
> *instead, called yourself*
> *a first generation free*

6. Heard "Liberté, égalité, fraternité"?

7. Did you know they stole
   that too?

Should've said you were just
borrowing   your brown
Said you were just stretching
                the truth
Said you were tired
of holding it all in
                your pockets
Sometimes the truth
is mistaken
                for a gun

8. Hadn't you fallen
   asleep yet?

9. Dreamt in American?

10. Awoken a swat vest Black
    average New York nigger
    a landing pad
    for nineteen muzzle flashes
    a hardworking bullseye?

11. Didn't your momma
    ever teach you how
    dangerous
    reaching
    can be?

The Time We Were Aliases

Josh, 15, ventures out. An adolescent need for speed. He forgoes dressing: white flag of a T-shirt and boxer shorts. He's not planning on stopping anywhere. Officers pull him over on the 91, between Compton and his home. Say he was driving twenty over the limit. Say he was swerving, but don't test his breath. They record his name as an alias for a fugitive of a similar name (different face, address, age, but similar name) wanted for grand theft auto. Josh, visibly shaken, denies any affiliation. Still booked. He is now Suspect. He calls his mother, but it's the middle of the night. It rings unanswered in the dark.

> We are silhouettes
> Bodies morphed into shadows
> Lost to the spotlight

Bell and Requiem

Tomorrow's Bells won't sound in glee
no bouquets tossed in midday air
no need to boast of bended knee
no pinned organza veiling hair

Her father's gift she will remain
no need to change a name for dance
the roses will not be in vain
but find themselves in mourning's stance

For his Nicole, no bride to be
won't hold his body hostage long
mascara turned to filigree
wrap his murder in unjust song

For every forget of his name
my dear, force-feed them all of his refrain

Freak Show Station

Hurry hurry!
Step right up
It's the most exciting
show in town   *I don't wanna watch*

Oscar Grant's death   Keep your arms and   *I don't wanna watch*
was recorded from   legs clear of the cage
multiple angles   Make sure not to step
by various BART   outside of the train
passengers

All are shaky   Sights, sounds   *What did you do*
                           wild things   *wrong?*
                           await you

in Blair Witch clarity   Please ladies and
Some have no sound   gentlemen
Some are a raging   No flash photography   *Somebody say*
cacophony of gasps   We don't want   *something*
and guns   to alarm the
                           bloodthirsty beasts
                           on the platform

                           Camera phones   *Why are we filming*
                           ready?   *this?*

15

Most sites that host
his handcuffed
heaven-send are
profitable

This next segment
may startle young
viewers
Are you ready to see
the greatest trick of
all?

Get off of him!
He didn't do anything
What are they doing?

on YouTube after
six-figure views

Watch a life
disappear before
your very eyes

Watch as subway
platform becomes
one-shot-stop
Watch a man soften
into a pile of forgotten
Please cover your ears
for the pop

Leave him alone!

He's already down

Why are their guns
drawn?
Stop!

Oscar Grant's death
has been enjoyed
over five million
times

Don't worry viewers
He will be fine
just sleeping off the
life

The first time
I watched
a man die

Don't mind the
trainers
Sometimes excessive

force is the only way
Don't forget to   I didn't share it
give them a good
review

Remember these are   Viral videos
just being broken in   I won't unsee

After all our infamy
depends on you

The Time We Went Over the Edge

Monday morning. Amandla is called to the school office. First thought: another surprise trip to Magic Mountain. Would the Viper push danger into her lungs again? When Josh told her someone died on it, she had laughed it off. Her mother quivers her signature, wipes tears, grabs Amandla's hand. Says she has packed her bag, but this doesn't feel like a vacation. Josh is in jail. Amandla snickers. Her usual role. *Mom, stop playing*. But Mom is locked in. No tears. Crying means believing. G-force pinning them along every curve of the 91. Each broken law its own death drop. Loop de loop. At the prison, her mother's pace burns grooves into the floor. Hours waiting in snaky lines. More hours begging them to run his prints. To clear his name. Premature verdict. Maximum security. Twin Towers Correctional. General population. No getting off. Her boy is not built for this.

Blurred hulks in twilight
Tracks swell toward endless downfall
Flagpoles pierce the heart

Sanford Sweet

2,487 miles

I remember the iced tea
we used to brew
on my mother's back
porch just outside her garden

How it steeped
against the ground
till deep-seated

How the sticky sweet
Alabama honey
stuck to our
everywhere

I wonder how hard
they had to scrub
to get the Trayvon off

Was it calm,
George,
calling it in?

Dream of Paradise
under an Arizona rainbow
sepia-ignorant bliss?

Whisper under breath
if we stack flowers at every site
this world can be Eden

again

I stand here
in the wilderness of kitchen
the linoleum tiles
a dry bubbling beneath
my bare feet

Our nursery
is quiet tonight
for all the right reasons
The eerie of crib mobile
plays soundtrack
to a muted television

Over a casket of
fruit spoiling before bite
under crescendo of kettle
in the most shameful
whisper say
I'm so glad we had
a girl

Summoning

1,996 miles

I got up early this morning, wore my woman today
Got up so early this morning, wore all my woman today
Though this sable seeped through, I thought I'd be safe

I held my baby's hand close, thought we'd be here for years
I, I, I, I held my baby's hand real close, thought we'd be here for years
But even standing this close, don't keep you free from fear

Thought he reached for his cell phone, don't know why he'd shoot
Saw him reach for his cell phone, God, why he'd shoot
Just being a mighty tree, is asking to tear out your roots

I ain't no gentlewoman, that's the honest truth
Now I wasn't a gentle woman, may be the honest truth
Hey, Hey, didn't make me bulletproof

(Don't know what I got to be who I got to be
God I will not be your next
of kin to #sayyourname)

The Time We Learned the Rules

Back of the courtroom. Mother and Amandla unwelcome flies on
the wall. Their sweaty palms. The creaking threat of being held in
contempt. The judge calls his name. Orange and filthy, a broken
oriole weighed down by chains. After seven days, did not know
how to lift his head. Amandla, just a chick herself, replaying
every rumble on the back porch. The adults holding court. Every
whisper that said he had always been rebellious, now this? The
judge raises his gavel. A moment released. No contest. Amandla
expects Mother to take flight to him. Swoop beneath his falling
body and give him rescue. But the door is open. She is gone.
Whistles for Amandla to come. That's not how freedom works.
You should know the rules by now.

//

Their parents take Josh and Amandla to a restaurant. Josh had
barely eaten, not bathed in a week. Local authorities enter. Sit
near the entrance of the establishment. Josh not done. At the
sight of the four uniformed patrolmen, Suspect sits up straight.
Goes silent. Slows to chew each bite like a leather bit. Looks at his
baby sister, Amandla, and swallows.

> Slow motion whiplash
> Hands held under the table
> We can't clean our plates

Gas Station Libretto

Jordan R. Davis—Teenage Passenger, Alto
Michael Dunn—Software Developer and Driver, Bass
Chorus of Three—Onlookers, Altos and Sopranos
Handgun—Veteran Instrument, Baritone

A gas station in Jacksonville, Florida; the day after
Thanksgiving.

(Handgun appears on stage dressed as an innocent bystander.
Begins the *Azione Teatrale* in falsetto.)

HANDGUN
Ladies and gentlemen!
Our actors are deep
in the turmoil of travel
when we find them
at the station
both have run empty
in need of refill
but not the same kind

Listen! Hark the bass
the incoming Durango
the roaring rap machine
plows into the scene
a vessel for the undoing

Then enter
from the west
the sputter of sedan
the silent carrier

Alas, my belly is beginning to
hunger and so it shall be full
once again

Mark this
the entrance of grief
the breath leaving
the journey has begun
heed its unraveling

(The thud and pulse of a loud car radio announces the entrance
of the players. Jordan, accompanied by three onlookers, bounce
in merriment on the wheels of a Dodge Durango looking to score
cigarettes and gum for the ride. Michael enters accompanied
by his swooning lover. They pull into the station to refresh
themselves with white wine and chips. It's 7:25 P.M. under a half
moon. Bass rattles both cars.)

HANDGUN
It begins! It begins!

(Michael approaches the Durango, swinging its passenger door
open. A bloom of red marches across his face. His hands a fury of
motion.)

CHORUS
(Piano decrescendo)

Calm down
It's only music
It's only music
Calm down

(Michael leans closer to the passenger. A sharp gesture aimed
at the sound system, then a jabbed finger at his own trembling
car.)

HANDGUN
And then the rise
What shall he say?

JORDAN
Who are you?
We don't have to turn down anything

(Slow piano crescendo; string section joins in diminished
chords. Michael, now burgundy mad, flails his arms, waves his
finger to condescend.)

JORDAN
What are you talking about?
(Michael rubs his skin as if in justification and mouths the
words *your kind* between staccato-horned expletives.)

JORDAN
Man, move around with that shit
Who do you think you're talking to?

(Piano crescendo, drums)

CHORUS
Stand down but
Stand your ground
Jordan, don't give up now

(Michael attempts to reach into the car, pushed back by chorus.)

JORDAN
Or else what?

(Michael calms, the red settles. His hands unball from fists. He becomes a pursed smile.)

JORDAN
I don't care who you are
I gotta right to play what I want

HANDGUN
(Laughing)

Come for me now
Let me show you
How a brute is awakened
How a line can't be uncrossed

a bell unrung
How to quiet a boy
without saying a word
Come now
for me

(Laughter of Handgun continues. Michael retreats out of sight.
Tension, a pulsing passenger.)

CHORUS
Stand your ground
Stand your ground
Jordan, don't give in

JORDAN
(In whistle register)
I won'—
(Ten shots, a rapid-fire kick bass, split the ear. Michael's shadow
backs away slowly.)

END

Filter

Before the airplane's wheels
kissed the tarmac goodbye
the story had changed twice:
      Black ~~son~~ ~~brother~~ boy
      ~~walking~~ ~~running~~ fleeing
      down the street with a ~~friend~~ ~~associate~~ accomplice
      when the police ~~agitated~~ ~~profiled~~ routinely stopped them
      in the nearby neighborhood of Ferguson, Missouri
      The officer ~~assumed~~ was notified
      of the ~~young man's~~ ~~teenager's~~ thug's involvement
      in a convenience store theft of ~~$2 tobacco~~, ~~cigarillos~~, cigars
      Witnesses say that the youth ~~surrendered to~~,
      ~~protected himself from~~ assaulted
      the officer provoking him to fire multiple shots
      into the ~~boy's~~ ~~unarmed~~ ~~still threatening~~ body

I sat with my cheek pressed
against the cold
double-paned window
checking if I could still
feel all of the
~~the living~~ the dying

I looked down below
hoping I could catch a glimpse
of the city ablaze
his name incensed on
our ~~angry~~ weary skin

His body lay there
all through my flight
a street spectacle
The neighbors pleaded
just to cover him in ~~decency~~ shame
His mother sobbing
as he puddled into
another stained pothole

Open Season

I have felt
the weather changing
falling leaves
painting the sidewalks
As a transplanted Texan
this hoof-printed fall
reminds me
hunting season has opened early

Every good hunter knows
you need
a good dog and a good gun
Get as close to your target as possible
make sure they can't see you clearly
this can be tricky
hunting through thicket

Don't bother
sitting on top of an open hill   (scan the forest
watching the surrounding pastures   through a scope)
and brushy banks
You're better inside the ~~hood~~ woods
So that if a ~~boy~~ buck
approaches
you can move back
stalk through cover

Dark fur
oversized antlers
the ones whose pelt sags
just below their waist
have the most tender innards
This one looked injured
dipped when he walked   (walk like a bandana
already took a shot at 'em   is weighing down
looked under 35   your back pocket)
That's good
Get 'em too old
they may have learned
how to run
how to stay quiet
invisible

Wanna guaranteed kill
use the envy of money
purchase a call
make it sound like a mother's voice
screaming out
Jesus!
or the ringing of Sean's wedding bells
My favorite sounds like a pretty girl
whispering "I love you"
anything that sounds familiar
or offers false hope

Once you got 'em in your crosshairs

Aim right under the hoodie

Stand your ground

Invite a friend

Tell 'em we don't shoot to eat

We will be legends

like Steve Irwin vs. Crocodile

                                        (Don't be quick be quiet

you saw this coming)

The Time We Were Thugs

Half a country away at college, Amandla receives a call from
back home. Mother. Says she and Father are okay. They are
okay. Says they were stopped tonight. On the back road behind
the church after service. After Father gave the benediction. A
blessing to hold for the week. Christmas play rehearsal went
well. Everyone was memorized. They are okay. Mother says she
swears, though Mother never swears. The officers saw the car.
The cocaine-white Lincoln on whitewalls. Heavy in the back
from the weight of a boy. One with a cap who lived close. They
offered him a ride home. The fog thick in those parts. They drove
slowly with no rush to be anywhere. Father now a senior citizen
and Mother with the top of the hill in sight. Police thought they
were a gang. From the rear window. Dreads. Afro. Baseball cap
cocked over do-rag like the local bangers. Too calm to be trusted.
After following them for blocks, the lights flashed on when they
crossed into unincorporated Perris. Both doors swung open
simultaneously. Guns drawn. Mother and Father's hands were
all you could see. Blinded by flashlights. Doors rocking on their
hinges. A livid breath held until the truth rose its head. Father
said he was a member of Cops and Clergy. Father said he was the
chaplain for the fire department. They ask him for his I.D. Then
they are a stuttering apology. A warning that a taillight can be
a death sentence. Mother says they are okay. They, buckled in
tighter amidst the thinning air and woodgrain, sang "We Shall
Overcome" to a wrenching silence. The boy made it home to
his grandmother. Amandla clinches the phone tighter. She has
studied for this test before.

Saying I'm okay
Over and over again
Only way to breathe

Tetras

We watched
your rise

to infamy, neon
through our cracks

our seams
pulled loose

Your swell has taught us
to school against blue

Trailing blood
we sunburst into captivity

Your cloaked batons
fashioned for our surrendered

already marked
hearts

You, Ferguson
the executioner's battleground

You,
the urban trench

Our gunpowder skin
makes the world

see flickers of us
Makes the world see us firework

monochromatic red,
You, sunken Independence Day.

Wolf Cry

1,623 miles

Before bedtime
my father's father would grab us
by the feet
tickle until
the laughter would stream from us

My father's rendition was to trap us
between his legs arrest our lungs
in the suspension of howl double us over
on the floor until we swore the wind wasn't in us

There was a father on the corner
when the CDs dropped
a snigger caught sneaking bread piece
no foul cry
no stop in sight

Until the cops
remembered theirs
brought the night early
held him until he cried
until his feet found no ground

Collapsed, deflated, a father
in fable, his oxen-blue
face

and we watched
and we watched

I cried
a sea of black
youth, that would never grow
into fathers
of anything

Kel-Tec PF-9

A rare piece of American history
released online for auction by the United Gun Group

The pistol procured by a former police officer, a bargain for any
connoisseur of American heartbreak

The firearm icon carries the case number from the battle of Trayvon
in permanent marker

While it is fairly young in age, it has seen its share of bloodshed
This item has already piqued the interest of many
police departments' training programs

Funds will be used to aid in the representation
of police officers appealing their wrongful death suits

Opening bid $100,000

Will appreciate
in value
with use

The Time We Came Close

There. Just past the suburbs they are building. May Ranch. On the
street just paved. But not yet painted. They will say she didn't stay
in her lane. That she slid into the intersection. Right where they
are putting in the street light. There is nothing there but dark
asphalt and an open field of alfalfa. Amandla. A California stop.
A seventeen-year-old and a back road after sunset. Did you hear
about the other girls? The ones the police made strip on the side
of the road? While they blocked traffic hiding their hands' caress
and deep dives? Over a dozen of them. They all started like this.
Amandla sits in her car. Alone. Her eyes wide. Officer darkens
the passenger-side window. Taps. A spotlight. She has to open
it. He leans so far in she can see his cavities. And all the things
he wants to fill. He asks how to get her home. Her heart audible.
Her finger a spinning compass. Sober. His lips drunk with power.
Officer opens door. Slides in. She, pressed against her door, fingers
gripping handle. She could carry her own weight in sprint down
the dirt road. He doesn't make her. This time is a warning. This
time is a slap on the wrist. This time.

> Not your enemy
> Forcibly you came for me
> You leave me no choice

Walmart Welcome

1,103 miles

Tape rolls and glass doors open wide
no sunshine welcome or recompense
track John's lawful aisle stride
I close my eyes and wince

No sunshine welcome or recompense
just motive on a guilty shelf
I close my eyes and wince
I confused you for myself

Just motive on a guilty shelf
four feet, no freeze, just instant shot
I confused you for myself
bleeding out and havoc wrought

Four feet, no freeze, just instant shot
tape rolls and glass doors open wide
bleeding out and havoc wrought
two threatening no-names dead inside

A Death Five Ways

1,271 miles

Hear lies	an unloaded toy
buoy of boy	rocked by see
cost for dreams	too much
rising to swell	collapse in his throat
brakes	the internet's sensation
our future	knows how to sailor
his blood	long enough to here
a passing bus	a stop too short
Tamired	to his own name

On Baltimore from Beeville

Work found us in Beeville
where the prison is currency
and the hotels give fresh cookies
to cut the taste of fear after six

The sun rose in the lobby
over Texas-shaped waffles
fruit loops, thick oatmeal, this town
no destination, reports the national news

Star-spangled birthplace finds
police officer unresponsive
after rioters attacked

Fires sparked
during the funeral
of Freddie Gray

(whom police left
to suffocate
under the weight of his own
body on the cold floor

of their van
while they watched
without response)

This is a test
This station is conducting a test
If this had been an actual emergency

Truckers mouth a murmured
slur over continental breakfast
of bleached biscuits
smothered in brown gravy
clench their fists
till purple pulses
around each knuckle

We sit at a separate
but equal banquette
chewing slowly
wondering what part of Texas
we waded into

Houston to Pool Party

270 miles

The stereotype speaks
We are more scared
of water than earth

I watched Dajerria
my little sister thirst
in a hot Texas
suburban wasteland

She gleamed of sweet
sweat sticky and
spilling poolside

towel around her shoulders
feet a shuffle of flip flop
and stalking sun

until they weren't

Snatch
a fourteen-year-old seaweed
suddenly replanted facedown in mud
under the stone of his knee
sun-scorched seedling
forced to shallow bloom

a grinding heave of lungs
filling with
unprovoked hate

a free-for-all
just not for us

The Time We Unlearned the Rules

A routine drive. Daylight. So much blooming up. Her Pontiac Sunfire sitting red against the bustling Galleria. Sage and Westheimer. Heavy traffic near the smoothie spots and cafés. Late enough for school to be out. Bright enough to remember clearly. A Mack Truck blocking an entire lane of traffic. No time for this. The sun is calling. She changes lanes, speeds to move around the commotion. Where there was emptiness there is now a man. She screeches to stop. Two hands slam down on the Sunfire's hood—enough to make a dent. Officer. Surely placed on street duty as punishment. He's yelling, cursing. Car horns bleat. Sidewalk in slow motion and full. The officer's face a red fury growing larger until he is the entire windshield. Amandla unthinking, finds herself out of the Sunfire. She's not a mother yet. *Why you hit my car? What is your badge number? GIVE ME YOUR BADGE NUMBER.* He swells at her chest. The car door stands open. The traffic cameras look the other way. Onlookers ready phones to record. Out of body, she watches it all. She and the officer. Middle of the street like a chalk outline. Close enough to spit, to shove, to kiss, to shoot.

> Tarred road gleams like ice
> Slack power lines now yanked taut
> Frog jumps out of pot

One Degree

Jeremyah says he met you
at a house party
Prairie View University
2013
between red cups
and Greek letters

Your hands held
an asylum of warmth
he still feels
when he drives
the road where you were taken
Says Bean may have known
you better

Bean says your name, Bland
was too familiar to hide
in the tall grass
Says you danced
your initials, S.B., into the
hardwood of the house
party I missed
Says we were the same
kind of wheat

I can still feel
the thrash
when we hold vigil

pray your name often
like a saint
or harvest

I let you in my soul
deeper than any good meal
or saving sentiment
can haunt

Release

When I decided to become a mother
people warned me
that having a child is forever
having your heart
floating around
outside your body

After birthing
two hatchlings
into the gulf
I know motherhood
is not being any less
than human
It is more about learning
to envelop the sea,
watching your skin
soft to slick to suckle to cradle
trading your blind spot
for the infinity of sightlines

Each surge of hormones
turning us more cephalopod,
and if I never believed in evolution
my daughter confirmed me a sea monster
My son made me more Ursula
a sea witch in drag

Did you know that an octopus has three hearts?
One to take all of the rejection life sends
the other two for the pearls we breathe for
My children's midnight risings are my palpitation
their tangled sleep is me wrestling my tentacles
The hardest part is not looking
away when I see my ink blooming in them

This world has tried to tell me
I can't have it all
the abyss and the surface too
I respond with my children's pyroclastic laughter

My confidence a constant in camouflage
my spirit has scraped the bottom
of the ocean more times than I want to admit
turning man into nightmare
and expectation into sinkhole

But my children give
the poor unfortunate of my soul
venom and a song
Give me a reason to unearth
myself from the sand every dawn
scheme us into a better sea

I wouldn't trade a limb for them, wouldn't beg
for bones or legs
but I am happy drowning
my sadness
in their saltwater cure

Did you know that a mother can swallow
a ship whole?
If you come for her offspring
she will drag you under
Davy Jones is a just woman
after too many miscarriages

When we have been stretched to distant oceans
when the pirates of work and school and sleep and stage
have stolen our collective chest bump, diverted
our propulsion
we be devilfish
lightly touching barbs
to get used to their cut

We are not hard
We are not a divided tether
We are an eight-legged doomsday
unfurling nets curled inside us
to seem larger than we are

Motherhood is a monstrosity waiting to surge:
It is a strangling safety
It is knowing
that you have all the reasons to whirlpool
and are just waiting for the moment
to release

And We Shake

After Hannah waited outside
an ally planted at the Waller County jail
80 days telling how the dirt still speaks

her name in hashtag
I mourn the tether of birth
I crave the picket

want to force them to say
how a body can hang and not stretch
a plastic noose

> *Hell you talmbout*
> *Hell you talmbout*

The Sheriff has already come for Hannah
her collar and his gun both bet
Jesus will protect them

My husband tells me not to go
our heir to consider
an unwanted goodbye in undertone

> *Hell you talmbout*
> *Hell you talmbout*

We offer my anger chilled
a bowl of fruit, cold, longing to quench
child in slumber, mother enraged

We barely make it to the cross street
before Hannah, now fire-engine fear
is running toward my driver's side window screaming
                    Don't stop here!

like she's seen a knight in gleaming hood
I accelerate, my foot deadweights
the grandfather's clock in my chest knows
the dogs are closing in
                    Say her name!

From the back seat
my daughter awakens in moan
                    What's happening?

Here, so close it could be our backyard
                    Say her name!

Here, a 30-minute drive from where I tuck her in with prayer
                    Say her name!

Here, where I now cower in a gas station parking lot
calculating if it is dark enough
to run

Don't

I have been to Prairie View before
Taken the road that bends
past the church, BBQ shack
don't know the street
name
but I know that tree

The one from the dash
cam
now covered in altar
candles
teddy bears, a wilted
flower's rumor

now tourist destination for the mourner
a reminder
of burning crosses

That tree: a lynching legacy
close to college dreams
surrealist hope

I try
to find where her
arm broke
backwards
and head pressed
easy
against the blurred limit

where the gust of
marching band plays
louder than I can lament

My feet stand at the curb
under the street lights
again
This time knowing
why it is dangerous for
them to burn out

The Pact

Even closer

Slit your wrists now Blend
your broken with mine
Us be family Have a pact
sealed in blood You will do it

Whichever of us they come for
next won't run or cower

See the red
scope light on you? See
how your chest welcomes
a sniper's round? Know
how much power lives
in blackout We can't shy away

Cut deep
into darkness Round the tendons
and muscle inside
your cheek Kiss me
death has a badge
and a reason to brandish

Hurry this urgency is a now kinda thing

We all gotta go
sometime Now it's promised
more swiftly It's now
or now we don't know no
never speak

our name Say we are
the same or fuck us

                                        I hope it's you
                                             just so
                                        it ain't me

Personal Effects

They will try to sell you
the myth of my lips
that I talked myself into more
trouble than my color could let
me live through

Try to convince you I knew
how to chameleon into two hours
of un-angled camera-feed static

With two hands mistook
myself for Hera dangled
myself from gold-chained plastic bags

They will try to say
I was quicksand
too much Texas
mud not enough blind
obey
My character
tin can on a backwoods fence

Tell them I never sat still
enough to be anyone's easy
target Tell them I have never
been able to stretch my lips
wide enough to swallow
my whole self This time

the body in the cell had no
holy water for spit
but had more God
in her than a Bible
Belt Make them wince
my name till it echoes
indictment

Teach them
we have always been
black magic
never intended to

The Time We Shook to Death

In the stretch of I-10 from Baton Rouge to Houston. Vidor.
Historical Bermuda triangle for all things black. Husband and
Amandla rushing back to watch their children rise for school. The
lights flick on just past city limits. Trained now. After Philando.
Amandla knows the drill. Hands on dash. Head bowed. Window
cracked just enough to be audible. Phone landscaped to cover the
widest terrain. Mothers are supposed to shield their children's
eyes when fathers expire before them. Her children are asleep
in their own beds, but her hands itch to press their lids closed
harder. She sees him laid before her. His last breath brushed
across her cheek. The officer shines in on her hands. Tells her
all of that is not necessary. Yes, she says. *It is*. She talks loud and
clear for the transcript to come. He runs his hand across the
butt of his gun. Then disappears. She and her husband are two
branches of the same road. She takes fear, he takes resolve. Asks
her why she is so afraid. He has reconciled death as ordained with
godly timing. She prays not to know God this way. The officer
returns with a warning for driving on the left too long. He tells
them to get right. Drives away. Amandla shakes through hours of
alternate endings. His hand in hers. Pulse elevated.

> Highways in moonlight
> How we tremble together
> This, the way we love

ACKNOWLEDGEMENTS

I am grateful to God first, for reasons that number like the stars themselves. I truly know humility through your work.

To my partner in life, Joshua, I am still unsure why you love me like I am a vessel for God's masterpieces. I am flawed for you. Thank you for always being willing to shake your head and smile.

Thank you to Olivet and Julius for giving me my voice back and giving up your time with mom.

To Phuc, Kate, and Jessica, thank you for believing in this work and for making a home for me at Bloomsday Literary. You kept the spirit of this book and pushed it to another level while lacing every edit with kindness and honesty in ways I never expected.

To my parents Patricia and Carl, thank you for believing in every word of every line and story. You were my first teachers and are my biggest cheerleaders.

To my older brother, Joshua, I have been and always am your biggest fan and fighter.

To Grandma Bettye, thank you for the prayers, the celebrations, the bragging and always reminding me that God favors your descendants the same way he favors you.

To Lupe and Jasminne, my first editors and dearest friends, thank you for every scolding encouragement and every kind critique.

You both are the masters of balance.

To Jordan, Monica, Rayla, Erica, Jeremyah, Bean, Dulcie and all of my Houston VIP Family, you have been my iron, forever sharpening.

Marcell, you were my first coach and you have never stopped making me better. Look at us now.

To Hannah, you are the reason I understand activism. I can never repay you for teaching me how to cross the line and still go home at the end of the day.

To Roger, Scott, Shanna, and every member of my Writer's Hotel cohort, thank you for all the feedback and honest reactions that helped shape this book.

For every family still waiting for justice, may you know that your loss is not in vain. May we say their names like royalty. May our ancestors lead the way to equality.

To every fan or reader that has supported my work whether written, on stage, in audio, or video, thank you for believing that one person and a bucket of words could shift this world even one degree off its axis.

Let's start the difficult conversations.

The text of *Newsworthy* is set using the family of Frutiger serif typefaces designed by Adrian Frutiger and Akira Kobayashi in 2008 based on the metal type version of Meridien.

CPSIA information can be obtained
at www.ICGtesting.com
Printed in the USA
FSHW010635241019
63323FS